THE TOP TEN
EVENTS
THAT CHANGED THE WORLD

Anita Ganeri

W
FRANKLIN WATTS
LONDON•SYDNEY

This edition published in the UK in 2011 by Franklin Watts

Franklin Watts
338 Euston Road
London NW1 3BH

Franklin Watts Australia
Level 17/207 Kent Street
Sydney, NSW 2000

Dewey classification: 303.4'8

A CIP catalogue record for this book is available from the British Library.

ISBN: 978 1 4451 0643 4

Franklin Watts is a division of Hachette Children's Books, an Hachette UK company.
www.hachette.co.uk

THE TOP TEN EVENTS THAT CHANGED THE WORLD
was produced for Franklin Watts by
David West Children's Books, 7 Princeton Court, 55 Felsham Road, London SW15 1AZ

Designer: Gary Jeffrey
Illustrator: David West
Editor: Katharine Pethick

Photographic credits:
7bl, David Friel; 15mt, TMWolf; 11b, 17b, Library of Congress; 20-21 all images courtesy of
NASA; 23m, White House Photo Office; 24, Remko van Dokkum; 25mt, U.S. Air Force
photo/Capt. Andy Biro; 25m, U.S. Air Force photo/Capt. Patrick Nichols; 25b, Photo by Derek
Jensen

Printed in China

Contents

INTRODUCTION
4

THE CRETACEOUS-
TERTIARY
EXTINCTION
EVENT
6

THE BLACK
DEATH
8

THE BOSTON
TEA PARTY
10

MOUNT
TAMBORA
ERUPTION
12

ASSASSINATION
OF ARCHDUKE
FERDINAND
14

PEARL HARBOR
16

HIROSHIMA
18

MOON LANDING
20

BERLIN WALL
COLLAPSE
22

9/11
24

THE BEST OF
THE REST
26

TIMELINE
30

GLOSSARY
31

INDEX
32

Introduction

The following events have been selected as the Top Ten from thousands of historical events that have undoubtedly changed our world. It is a horribly difficult choice to make when there are so many events to pick from. So why have these ten made it into the book, and not others that seem equally important?

✱ Firstly, the event must have affected the entire world, not just a part of it.

✱ Secondly, it must have had an impact on the world within a reasonably short space of time. (The Ice Age, for example, does not make the Top Ten because it happened over a longer period of time.)

The last Ice Age is an example of an important event that affected most of our world. Unfortunately, it also unfolded too slowly to be included in our list.

The San Francisco earthquake and fire of 1906 was a momentous event but only directly affected the USA.

The bombing of civilians in Guernica, during the Spanish Civil War (1936–1939), caused outrage but this event has not shaped the modern world.

✳ Thirdly, it must still affect our lives today in the way it has helped to shape the modern world.

You might disagree with some of the events that have been chosen here. In which case, you might like to put together your own list of important events.

The Cretaceous-Tertiary Extinction Event

Around 65 million years ago, dinosaurs roamed the world, the oceans teemed with life, and pterosaurs flew through the skies. Then came an event so cataclysmic that 80 per cent of all animal species on Earth perished. Many people believe that the cause of this mass extinction was a meteorite – a piece of rock from space that survived the journey through the Earth's atmosphere to collide with the Earth at huge speed. Such an impact would have sent so much rock and dust into the atmosphere that the whole world would have been plunged into darkness for months.

Proof of the impact is clearly visible in rocks in certain places. The event layer is rich in iridium, a mineral found in meteorites.

AN EXTINCTION DISASTER

There is much evidence to support the meteorite-strike theory. A huge crater more than 180 kilometres in diameter has been discovered in the Yucatan Peninsula in Mexico. The crater, known as the Chicxulub crater after the present-day town near its centre, seems to have been created by an impact at the end of the Cretaceous period – 65 million years ago. The collision of the meteorite also seems to have caused widespread wildfires and gigantic tsunamis. All of the dinosaurs, except for the archosaurs, disappeared after this time, as did many types of marine life and the pterosaurs, in **one of the most massive extinctions of all time. The survivors effectively were left to inherit the Earth.**

Meteorite splinters may have struck the Moon, causing craters like the Tycho crater, which is visible on the Moon's surface and is probably the result of an asteroid impact over 100 million years ago.

Crocodilians such as this gharial have evolved from survivors of the mass extinction.

Without competition mammals were able to evolve into new types like bats to fill the empty skies.

Would hominins, who gave rise to humans, have evolved in a dinosaur dominated world?

Birds are the only living descendants of the dinosaurs.

The Black Death

The early 1300s were hard years for Europe. Food shortages and rising prices resulted in a terrible famine that lasted from 1315 to 1317. Meanwhile a deadly, infectious disease – bubonic plague – was racing along the trade routes from the East. In 1347, it reached the Crimea and was then carried back to Europe by traders. The vast, undernourished populations of Europe were defenceless against it. The plague took hold in Italy, with victims rarely living for more than three days after infection. It probably got its name, the Black Death, from the black colour of a victim's skin just before death. For three years, it ravaged Western Europe, terrorising towns and wiping out whole communities. It is estimated that the population of Europe was reduced by about one-third and that 25 million people died as a result of the Black Death.

Bubonic plague was a highly infectious disease, caused by a bacterium carried in the blood of fleas that lived on black rats. When the rats died, the fleas bit humans and infected them. Symptoms included fever, vomiting and swelling.

THE GRIM REAPER

To the survivors of the plague outbreak the world would never be the same again. Before the Black Death, the feudal system tied peasants to working for a particular landowner. But the high number of plague deaths resulted in a massive labour shortage. Now peasants could choose to work for the highest bidder, bringing the feudal system to an end. The experience of the plague also led to a whole new way of thinking about humanity and its place in the world. People lost faith in the Church. They married later, had fewer children and lived for the moment. **In many countries, art, sculpture and literature reflected people's preoccupation with death and what happened after death.**

Plague doctors wore masks and long robes to try to protect themselves from infection.

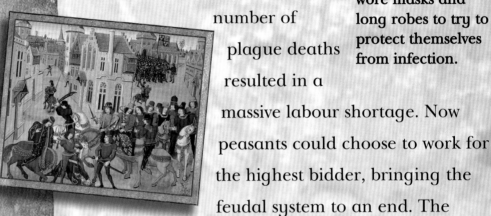

In 1381, peasants in England rose up in rebellion. They were angry at the king's attempts to remove some of the rights they had gained after the end of the Black Death.

Lady Luck spins her wheel, a scene from *The Decameron* (1353), a book of stories inspired by the Black Death.

The Boston Tea Party

On a cold December evening in 1773, a group of around 200 men, some disguised in Indian costume, headed towards Griffin's Wharf in Boston harbour, North America. They boarded three tea ships that were moored there, and quickly began to break open the chests of tea that were loaded on the ships. The tea and the chests were dumped over the side into the waters of the harbour. Once the ships were emptied of tea, the men slipped quietly away. This was the so-called Boston Tea Party. The actions of the American colonists who dumped the 342 chests of tea were intended to send a clear message to the British government – we will not pay your taxes!

PRELUDE TO A WAR

In 1763, Britain was victorious in the French and Indian War. But the war had been extremely costly. The British government decided to raise some cash by taxing its American colonies.

The hated British Parliament

Several new taxes were introduced, including one on tea. The colonists were furious because they had no representatives in the British Parliament. To make matters worse, in 1773 the British government passed the Tea Act. It gave the East India Company a monopoly on tea imported into the colonies.

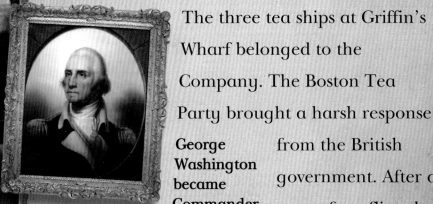

The colonists formed local militias to fight the British.

The three tea ships at Griffin's Wharf belonged to the Company. The Boston Tea Party brought a harsh response from the British government. After a year of conflict, the colonists declared independence on 4 July 1776.

George Washington became Commander-in-Chief of the American forces when war broke out in 1775.

Five years later, they had beaten the British. **In 1789, George Washington, the first president of the United States of America, was sworn in.**

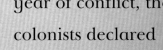

Signing of The American Constitution in 1787

Mount Tambora Eruption

Mount Tambora, on the island of Sumbawa in Indonesia, was a giant volcano soaring 4,300 metres into the sky. It had been silent for many thousands of years – until 1815. On 5 April of that year, people living more than 1,000 kilometres from the volcano reported hearing explosions that sounded like cannon fire. These small eruptions, however, were only warning signals of the cataclysm to come. Six days later, onlookers witnessed 'three columns of fire rising to a great height'. A massive eruption sent 50 cubic kilometres of magma shooting out of Mount Tambora, plunging Sumbawa and islands hundreds of kilometres away into pitch darkness. Flows of hot ash and gas surged down Tambora's slopes at terrifying speeds, burying and burning everything in their path. The ash fell into the sea, setting off gigantic tsunamis that engulfed neighbouring islands. At least 10,000 people died in the disaster that day.

The massive eruption removed 1,450 metres of Mount Tambora's summit. The explosion also created a vast crater 6 by 7 kilometres wide and 1 kilometre deep in the top of the volcano.

Pieces of pumice measuring 20 centimetres across rained down.

Europe suffered widespread crop failures, just as it was recovering from the devastation of the Napoleonic Wars.

VOLCANIC WINTER

Over 200 million tonnes of sulphur dioxide gas were launched into the Earth's atmosphere as a result of the eruption, reflecting sunlight away from the Earth. Global temperatures fell by as much as 3°C, and the year 1816 became known as the 'year without a summer', when snow fell during June and frost was still widespread in July. In the worst famine of the 19th century, hundreds of thousands of people died. In some places, people were reduced to eating rats and farmers were murdered by famished mobs as they took their produce to market. **All of these factors made Mount Tambora the first modern disaster to affect the entire planet.**

Could it happen again? It did – in 1991, Mount Pinatubo in the Philippines erupted for the first time in 600 years. Luckily around 200,000 people were evacuated before the volcano blew.

The Assassination of Archduke Ferdinand

Two gunshots fired on a June morning in Sarajevo, the capital of Bosnia, helped to change the course of history. The shots were fired by 19-year-old Gavrilo Princip, a member of a Serbian revolutionary group, the Black Hand, who was aiming at Archduke Franz Ferdinand and his wife Sophie, during an official visit to Sarajevo. Having just survived one assassination attempt that day, they were leaving the city when their open-topped car was forced to slow down at a sharp turn. The Archduke and his wife were killed almost instantly.

THE GREAT WAR

Archduke Franz Ferdinand was the heir to the throne of Austro-Hungary.

A 1916 German hand grenade

The Black Hand chose him as a target because they were unhappy about Austro-Hungarian influence in the Balkan states. However, the assassination gave Austro-Hungary the excuse it wanted to open hostilities against Serbia. Austro-Hungary held the Serbian government responsible for the actions of the Black Hand and declared war on Serbia in July 1914. The knock-on effects were immediate. Russia was bound by treaty to come to Serbia's aid, and it mobilised its army. Germany declared war on Russia. France and Britain both declared war on Germany.

World War I is remembered for its trench warfare in which many thousands of men died.

War machines developed quickly, giving rise to the world's first fighter aircraft and tanks.

World War I had started, sparked by Princip's fateful shots.

No other war had changed the map of Europe so dramatically. The peace treaty also sowed the seeds for World War II to come.

EUROPE 1919

TREATY OF PEACE

THE ALLIED AND ASSOCIATED POWERS
AND
GERMANY,

The Protocol annexed thereto, the Agreement respecting the military occupation of the territories of the Rhine, AND THE
TREATY
BETWEEN
FRANCE AND GREAT BRITAIN
RESPECTING
Assistance to France in the event of unprovoked aggression by Germany.

Signed at Versailles, June 28th, 1919.

Pearl Harbor

It was 7.55 am on a peaceful Sunday morning at the US Command Center on Ford Island in Pearl Harbor, Hawaii. Commander Logan C Ramsey spotted the approach of a low-flying plane, then he saw 'something black fall out of that plane'. It was a bomb. Immediately, Ramsey radioed a message to every US ship and base – 'Air raid on Pearl Harbor' – but it was already too late. The Japanese attack on the US naval base at Pearl Harbor was a complete surprise and caused utter chaos. In only two hours, two waves of bombing destroyed a large part of the US Pacific Fleet as well as more than 180 aircraft and left around 2,300 people dead.

A GIANT AWAKENS

Tensions between the USA and Japan had increased when Japan became allies with the Axis powers (Germany and Italy) in 1940. The attack on Pearl Harbor was intended to cripple the US Pacific Fleet and to open up the way for Japan's invasion of Southeast Asia.

President Franklin D. Roosevelt signed the declaration of war against Japan the day after the Pearl Harbor attacks.

This wartime propaganda poster urged the American people to remember the Pearl Harbor attacks.

Before Pearl Harbor, the majority of the US public did not want to become involved in the war that was being fought between the Allies (Britain, France and the Soviet Union) and the Axis powers. But the attack caused a massive swing in public opinion. The next day, the USA declared war on Japan, prompting Germany to declare war on the USA. **The attack on Pearl Harbor brought the USA into World War II, changing the course of history.**

The American airforce joined the Allies in the fight against the Axis Powers in Europe and elsewhere.

American troops helped to liberate Paris, France from German control in 1945.

Hiroshima

Early on the morning of 6 August 1945, the B-29 bomber Enola Gay took off from the island of Tinian in the West Pacific. The pilot, Colonel Paul Tibbets, set a course for the city of Hiroshima in Japan. On board his plane, he had the most powerful bomb known to humans, an atomic bomb with the codename 'Little Boy'. Tibbets took the bomber up to 9,500 metres above the city before dropping the bomb at 8.15 am. The bomb took about 50 seconds to reach its detonation height, roughly 600 metres above the city. The explosion rocked the Enola Gay, which was already several kilometres away, and sent a huge mushroom cloud up into the air. It destroyed 10 square kilometres of the city and instantly killed an estimated 66,000 people. Thousands more died later from radiation poisoning.

The human cost of conquering islands like Iwo Jima showed the Japanese army was determined to fight to the bitter end, for years if necessary.

The atomic bomb dropped on Hiroshima had a force equal to more than 15,000 tonnes of TNT.

NUCLEAR DAWN

World War II in Europe had finally ended on 8 May 1945. But it was not finished in the Pacific. British and American forces continued to fight the Japanese. The United States, however, had a secret and devastating weapon at their disposal. The atomic bomb was first tested in July 1945, and the bombing of Hiroshima was the first use of a nuclear weapon. On 15 August, Japan finally surrendered, bringing World War II to an end. **Hiroshima ushered in the nuclear age, which saw the beginning of the Cold War and promised cheap, renewable energy for the future.**

A second atomic bomb was dropped on the Japanese city of Nagasaki on 9 August 1945.

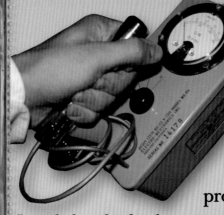

It took decades for the radiation in Hiroshima to fall to safe levels.

Nuclear power can be safely used to generate electricity.

Fearsome Cold War weapons like this Trident missile represent the ever present threat of nuclear war.

1969

Moon Landing

'I believe this nation should commit itself to achieving the goal, before this decade is out, of landing a man on the Moon and returning him safely to the Earth.' So spoke US President John F. Kennedy in a speech in May 1961. Two years later, the president was dead but his dream was realised in 1969, when the Eagle lunar lander touched down on the surface of the Moon. It is estimated that 500 million people all over the world watched on their TV screens as astronaut Neil Armstrong took the first step on to the dusty lunar surface, uttering the famous words: 'That's one small step for [a] man, one giant leap for mankind.'

The last Moon landing, Apollo 17 in 1972, made use of a lunar rover vehicle.

THE SPACE RACE

The Moon landing proved a victory for the USA in the 'space race' between the USA and the USSR. The Soviets had successfully launched the first satellite, Sputnik 1, into space in 1957 and had put the first man, Yuri Gagarin, into orbit around Earth in 1961. However, after the success of the Apollo 11 mission, international cooperation began to become a feature of space exploration. In 1975, the USA and the USSR launched a joint Apollo-Soyuz mission. Since then, astronauts of many different nationalities have visited the International Space Station. **The** impact of the Moon landing had made the dream of space exploration a reality.

The Soviet satellite Sputnik 1 was launched in 1957.

The US space shuttle made its first mission in 1981. It was the world's first reusable spacecraft.

The explosion of the space shuttle Challenger in 1986 affected public confidence in space flight.

Successors of SpaceShipOne will take paying passengers into space.

The construction of the International Space Station has been ongoing since 1998.

Berlin Wall Collapse

Since 1961, the wall built across the city of Berlin had cruelly divided families and friends in two. Thousands of people had risked their lives crossing the Wall from East to West Germany. Many had been captured or killed in the attempt. But in the autumn of 1989, things began to change. On 9 November, the East German government lifted restrictions on travel to West Germany. Huge crowds of people gathered along the Wall, demanding to be allowed through the crossing points. One by one, the gates were opened and crowds of East Germans surged through. Many people climbed on to the hated Wall; others began to remove chunks from it. The Berlin Wall had fallen.

US and Soviet tanks face each other at Checkpoint Charlie, just two months after the construction of the Berlin Wall started in 1961.

DIVIDED WE FALL

When World War II ended in 1945, Berlin became a focus for Cold War tensions between the communist Soviet and Western powers. In 1949, Germany was divided into the communist-controlled German Democratic Republic (East Germany) and the Federal Republic of Germany (West Germany). Over the next few years, thousands of people left East Germany for the West. East Germany gradually closed its borders, until Berlin remained the only route to the West. The Berlin Wall was built to stop people leaving. Its destruction came as a result of the political changes of the late 1980s when Soviet leader Gorbachev brought in much needed social and economic reforms (called perestroika). **After 42 years Germany was reunited and the Cold War, which had brought the world to the brink of destruction, was finally ended in 1991.**

The Berlin Airlift delivered supplies to the residents of the Western-controlled sectors of Berlin during the Soviet blockade of 1948–9.

Soviet leader Mikhail Gorbachev (right) and US president Ronald Reagan.

A Soviet postage stamp promoting the idea of perestroika – 'restructuring' or reform.

Driving humble Trabants, thousands of East Germans crossed into West Germany after the fall of the Wall.

9/11

On a cloudless, blue-sky day in New York City, onlookers stood stunned and shocked. At 8.46 am on 11 September 2001, a large plane flew directly into the north tower of the famous World Trade Center. At first people were unsure whether they had witnessed an accident. But when a second plane crashed into the south tower only 15 minutes later, it became clear that these were deliberate acts. In fact, four planes had been hijacked that morning by 19 attackers, all associated with the extreme Islamic group Al-Qaeda. The third plane hit the headquarters of the US Department of Defense, the Pentagon, at 9.40 am. A little later a fourth plane crashed in the countryside in Pennsylvania. It seems that its passengers, alerted by mobile calls to what was happening, had tried to overpower their attackers.

Pedestrians fleeing from the thick dust cloud created by the collapse of the Twin Towers.

'WAR ON TERROR'

President George W. Bush announces the US response to the terrorist attacks.

Nearly 3,000 people died in the 9/11 attacks. The attacks were condemned by people all around the world, many of whom had watched in disbelief as the horrific events unfolded on their television screens. The attacks soon had far-reaching consequences for countries far from the United States. The fight against terrorism became a top priority for US president George Bush and his government, and the search for members of Al-Qaeda intensified. However, the headquarters of Al-Qaeda was in Afghanistan. When the Taliban government refused to cooperate with the United States, or to hand over Osama bin Laden, the leader of Al-Qaeda, US and allied forces launched the 'war on terror' in October 2001. **Since 9/11, terrorism has become one of the major dangers facing the world.**

Fires still raged at 'Ground Zero' – the site where the Twin Towers collapsed – three days after the attack.

The US military began the 'war on terror' in Afghanistan with bombing raids.

Two beams of light showed where the Twin Towers stood in the 2004 memorial.

The Best of the Rest

FIRST CRUSADE 1095

An illuminated manuscript shows a scene from the First Crusade.

The crusades were military campaigns organised by Christian Europe. The Christians wanted to stop the spread of Islam, and to recapture the Holy Land – a region that included many sites sacred to Christians – from Muslim control. The first Crusade began after Pope Urban II called on Christians to fight a war against the Turks. After three years and a long siege, the Christians finally succeeded in capturing Jerusalem. The crusades went on for another 200 years, and changed European society for ever, encouraging trade and slowing the advance of Muslim power.

FRENCH REVOLUTION 1789

In 1789, the people of France rose up against their king, Louis XVI. The French peasants were heavily taxed, and angry.

Model of a revolutionary era guillotine

A disastrous harvest in 1788 had left many hungry. On 14 July, a crowd attacked the Bastille prison in Paris – a symbol of the power of the king. In August, the French National Assembly passed the 'Declaration of the Rights of Man and of the Citizen', promising the French people that they would now be citizens, not subjects of a monarch. The royal family was arrested, and the king was beheaded in 1793. The Revolution led to six years of civil war until Napoleon Bonaparte seized power in 1799.

HAITIAN REVOLUTION 1791

At the time of the French Revolution, Saint-Domingue, an island in the Caribbean, was France's most profitable colony, producing 40 per cent of the world's sugar. Its sugar plantations were worked by black slaves from West Africa. In 1791, there was a slave revolt on the island during which a former slave, called Toussaint l'Ouverture emerged as leader. In 1801, Toussaint declared himself governor of the island.

But Napoleon Bonaparte sent troops to reclaim the island. Toussaint died in 1803, but in 1804, the French forces were defeated and Saint-Domingue became the independent republic of Haiti.

The sinking of the Lusitania was considered an outrage. The killing of prominent American citizens by the Germans had a profound effect.

SINKING OF THE LUSITANIA 1915

On 1 May 1915, the British ocean liner Lusitania left pier 54 in New York City, USA, carrying nearly 2,000 passengers to Liverpool. Many passengers were nervous – Britain was at war with Germany and the Germans had declared the waters around Britain a war zone. On 7 May, the Lusitania was hit by a torpedo fired by a German U-boat and sank in 20 minutes off the south coast of Ireland. Of the 1,198 lives lost, 128 were US citizens. The sinking of the liner caused outrage in the United States, and was one of the reasons for the later entry of the United States into World War I in 1917.

This painting depicts the Haitian revolution in full swing. It was the first time slaves had revolted successfully for a lasting freedom.

RUSSIAN REVOLUTION 1917

The Russian Revolution was really two revolutions – the first in February 1917 overthrew the tsar, and the second in October put a Bolshevik (communist) in power. World War I saw the Russian army suffering terribly in campaigns against Germany and at home the Russian people were suffering food shortages. Imperial rule ended when a revolt forced Tsar Nicholas II to abdicate. The provisional government was then overthrown by the Bolshevik Party led by Vladimir Lenin. The revolution led to civil war, and finally to the creation of the Soviet Union.

Vladimir Lenin, leader of the October revolution

THE WALL STREET CRASH 1929

During the 1920s, the value of stocks and shares in the USA kept rising. Many people used savings, or borrowed money, to buy and sell stocks and shares to make a profit. In September 1929, the price of stocks and shares began to go down and suddenly people had to sell their investments. 24 October, known as Black Thursday, saw the start of a huge rush to sell which led to the market 'crash' as stocks and shares lost nearly half of their value. This was the start of the Great Depression, during which companies had to close and thousands of people were out of work. It lasted for 10 years and affected countries worldwide.

A victim of the Great Depression

CUBAN MISSILE CRISIS 1962

The missile crisis was a major confrontation between the USA and the USSR. The USSR supported the communist regime of Fidel Castro in Cuba. In July 1962, the Soviets began to ship ballistic missiles to Cuba, determined to help defend the island.

The USA shows evidence of Cuban missiles to the United Nations.

If fired from Cuba, the missiles could have hit the USA in minutes. US president John F. Kennedy set up a blockade to prevent the Soviets delivering more missiles. Tension between the two superpowers grew and the world was on the brink of nuclear war until Soviet leader Nikita Khrushchev withdrew the missiles.

MARTIN LUTHER KING'S WASHINGTON SPEECH 1963

'I have a dream that one day this nation will rise up and live out the true meaning of its creed: 'We hold these truths to be self-evident, that all men are created equal.' More than 200,000 people heard the civil rights activist Martin Luther King deliver these words as part of his most famous speech.

Luther King's speech was a rallying cry for racial integration.

King's 'I have a dream' speech took place in Washington DC, on 28 August 1963. The March on Washington was organised to demand equal justice for citizens of all races. Martin Luther King was killed by a sniper's bullet in 1968.

IRANIAN REVOLUTION 1979

In January 1978, Iran was rocked by demonstrations against its monarch, Shah Mohammad Reza Pahlavi. Many protesters supported the Islamic cleric Ayatollah Khomeini, who had been in exile since 1964.

The effects of the Iranian revolution are still being felt today.

The protests and strikes continued despite government efforts to quell them. In January 1979, the shah was forced to flee the country. Two weeks later, crowds welcomed Ayatollah Khomeini back to Iran. Government troops were overthrown and Khomeini declared Iran to be an Islamic Republic.

INDIAN OCEAN EARTHQUAKE 2004

On 26 December 2004, an underwater earthquake off the coast of Sumatra, in Indonesia, set off a gigantic tsunami. Over the next seven hours, the series of gigantic waves travelled thousands of kilometres across the Indian Ocean, devastating coastal areas when they made landfall. This catastrophic tsunami killed at least 225,000 people in Indonesia, Sri Lanka, India, the Maldives and Thailand.

Indonesia was one of many countries devastated by the 2004 tsunami.

WORLD FINANCIAL CRISIS 2008

The financial crisis began in 2007, when house prices in the USA dropped rapidly. This then affected banks, mortgage-lenders and insurance companies. Many businesses, who could no longer borrow money from their ailing banks, collapsed. The crisis spread around the world. In 2008 stock markets crashed and banks were bailed out by governments. The resulting recession is the worst since the 1930s.

Timeline of Events

		The Event	What Happened
PRE-HISTORY	205 Ma	THE TRIASSIC-JURASSIC EXTINCTION EVENT	Massive volcanic eruptions which created floods of lava and released greenhouse gases.
	65 Ma	**THE CRETACEOUS–TERTIARY EXTINCTION EVENT**	**It is thought that a meteorite hit the Earth, creating a dust cloud that blocked out the sun.**
	2.58 Ma	THE ICE AGE	Ice sheets and glaciers covered large parts of the Earth's surface.
ANCIENT	3000 BC	EGYPT IS UNIFIED	Lower and Upper Egypt became a unified state.
	753 BC	ROME IS FOUNDED	Legendary founding date of the city of Rome.
	30 BC	THE BIRTH OF JESUS CHRIST	Jesus of Nazareth, believed by Christians to be the Son of God, was born in Bethlehem, Judea.
MEDIEVAL	1095	THE FIRST CRUSADE	A military campaign by European Christians to reclaim the Holy Land from Muslim control.
	1347	**THE BLACK DEATH**	**The plague was carried along trade routes from Asia to Europe, reaching Europe in 1347.**
	1492	DISCOVERY OF THE NEW WORLD BY CHRISTOPHER COLUMBUS	Italian sailor Christopher Columbus sailed west from Spain across the Atlantic Ocean.
MODERN	**1773**	**THE BOSTON TEA PARTY**	**American colonists dumped cargoes of tea into Boston harbour in protest over taxes.**
	1789	FRENCH REVOLUTION	The French people overthrew the royal family.
	1791	HIATIAN REVOLUTION	There was a slave revolt on Saint-Domingue.
	1815	**MOUNT TAMBORA**	**The volcano erupted, killing 10,000 people instantly and 82,000 died as a result of ashfall.**
20TH CENTURY–	**1914**	**ASSASSINATION OF ARCHDUKE FERDINAND**	**Gavrilo Princip assassinated Archduke Franz Ferdinand and his wife Sophie in Sarajevo.**
	1915	SINKING OF THE LUSITANIA	A German U-boat sank the British ocean liner off the coast of Ireland, killing 1,198 people.
	1917	RUSSIAN REVOLUTION	The tsar was overthrown.
	1929	WALL STREET CRASH	The value of stocks and shares dropped suddenly.
	1941	**PEARL HARBOR**	**The Japanese attacked the US Pacific fleet in Pearl Harbor, Hawaii.**
	1945	**HIROSHIMA**	**A US B-29 bomber dropped the first atomic bomb on the Japanese city of Hiroshima.**
	1963	CUBAN MISSILE CRISIS	Soviet plans for ballistic missiles in Cuba brought conflict between the US and the USSR.
		WASHINGTON SPEECH	Speech calling for equal rights for all races.
	1969	**APOLLO 11 MOON LANDING**	**Neil Armstrong was the first man on the Moon.**
	1979	IRANIAN REVOLUTION	The Shah fled Iran and Ayatollah Khomeini returned from exile.
	1989	**FALL OF THE BERLIN WALL**	**Crossings in the Berlin Wall were opened.**
	2001	**THE 9/11 TERROR ATTACKS**	**Al-Qaeda terrorists highjacked planes, and flew two into New York's twin towers.**
	2004	INDIAN OCEAN EARTHQUAKE	A massive earthquake set off a huge tsunami.
	2008	GLOBAL FINANCIAL CRISIS	Falling US house prices were the start of the financial crisis.

Glossary

What Changed

The event killed roughly 50 per cent of all species on Earth.
The event killed off the dinosaurs.

The world's climate was cooler and drier than the climate today.

The dynastic period in Egyptian history began.
The ancient Romans built a powerful empire.
Christianity went on to become a major world religion.

After three years of fighting, the Christians reconquered Jerusalem.
The plague killed one-third of Europe's population.
The 'discovery' of the New World opened up the Americas to European exploration.

The British government's response helped set the British and colonists on the path to war.
The Revolution resulted in civil war, which ended when Napoleon Bonaparte seized power.
Resulted in the independence of Haiti in 1804.
The eruption affected the world climate, causing the 'year without a summer' (1816).

The assassination set in motion a series of events that led to the start of World War I.
The sinking was one of the factors that led to the United States entering World War I in 1917.
Revolution led to the communist Soviet Union.
The crash resulted in the Great Depression.
The attack brought the United States into World War II.
A second bomb was dropped on Nagasaki and the Japanese surrendered, ending World War II.
The world was on the brink of nuclear war until the USSR backed down.
Speech changed the course of human rights.
Encouraged investment in space science.
Ayatollah Khomeini declared the Islamic Republic of Iran. War with Iraq followed.
East and West Germany were united again.
US president Bush launched a 'war on terror' against Al-Qaeda in Afghanistan.
225,000 died and coastal areas were devastated.
Financial crisis spread worldwide, affecting banks and businesses in many countries.

atomic bomb A weapon that explodes as a result of nuclear fission

Balkan states The countries that lie in the Balkan peninsula in southeast Europe

bankruptcy A legal state in which a person or business is unable to pay their creditors

Cold War The state of conflict and tension that existed between the USA and the USSR from the mid 1940s until the early 1990s

feudal system The medieval system that tied peasants to work for a particular manor and lord

militia A military force made up of citizens

monopoly Describes a situation when a person or a business has sole control over a particular service or product

propaganda Information aimed at influencing the way people think and behave

space race The race between the USA and the USSR to be the first in space

torpedo A self-propelled weapon that can be fired through the air or underwater and is designed to explode on impact

tsunami A giant wave caused by the movement of an undersea earthquake

uranium A heavy, silvery-white metal that is used as a fuel in a nuclear reactor

Index

A

Al-Qaeda, 24, 25
Armstrong, Neil, 20
Atomic bombs, 18, 19

B

Berlin Wall, fall of, 22, 23
Bin Laden, Osama, 25
Black Death, 8, 9
Black Hand, 14, 15
Boston Tea Party, 10, 11
Bubonic plague, 8, 9
Bush, George W, 25

C

Chicxulub crater, Mexico, 7
Cold War, 19
Cretaceous-Tertiary
    extinction event, 6, 7
Crusades, 26
Cuban Missile Crisis, 28

D

Dinosaurs, 6, 7

E

Earthquakes,
    Indian Ocean, 29
    San Francisco, 4
Enola Gay, 18

F

Ferdinand, Archduke
    Franz, 14, 15
French Revolution, 26

G

Gagarin, Yuri, 21
Gorbachev, Mikhail, 23

H

Haitian Revolution, 26
Hiroshima, 18, 19

I

Ice Age, 4
Iranian Revolution, 29

K

Kennedy, John F, 20
King, Martin Luther, 28

L

Lusitania, sinking of, 27

M

Meteorite strike, 6, 7
Moon landing, 20, 21

N

9/11, 24, 25

P

Pearl Harbor, 16, 17
Pinatubo, eruption of, 13
Princip, Gavrilo, 14, 15

R

Reagan, Ronald, 23
Roosevelt, Franklin D, 17
Russian Revolution, 27

S

Space race, 21
Space station,
    International, 21
Sputnik 1, 21

T

Tambora, eruption of Mt,
    12, 13
Tsunamis, 7, 12, 29

W

Wall Street Crash, 28
Washington, George, 11
World financial crisis, 29
World War I, 15
World War II, 15, 16, 17,
    18, 19, 23